# TINY HOUSE

Think Small! An Introduction to Tiny House Living

(How to Downsize to Save Money and Space)

**Luann Coleman**

Published by Tomas Edwards



*Tiny House: Think Small! An Introduction to Tiny House*

*Living (How to Downsize to Save Money and Space)*

ISBN 978-1-990373-03-9

**Legal & Disclaimer**

The information contained in this book is not designed to replace or take the place of any form of medicine or professional medical advice. The information in this book has been provided for educational and entertainment purposes only.

The information contained in this book has been compiled from sources deemed reliable, and it is accurate to the best of the Author's knowledge; however, the Author cannot guarantee its accuracy and validity and cannot be held liable for any errors or omissions. Changes are periodically made to this book. You must consult your doctor or get professional medical advice before using any of the suggested remedies, techniques, or information in this book.

Upon using the information contained in this book, you agree to hold harmless the Author from and against any damages, costs, and expenses, including any legal fees potentially resulting from the application of any of the information provided by this guide. This disclaimer applies to any damages or injury caused by the use and application, whether directly or indirectly, of any advice or information presented, whether for breach of contract, tort, negligence, personal injury, criminal intent, or under any other cause of action.

You agree to accept all risks of using the information presented inside this book. You need to consult a professional medical practitioner in order to ensure you are both able and healthy enough to participate in this program.

# Table of Contents


INTRODUCTION........................................................1

CHAPTER 1: THE BLUEPRINT.............................4

CHAPTER 2: CONVERTED HOMES ....................10

CHAPTER 3: WHAT ARE TINY HOUSES?...........24

CHAPTER 4: WHAT ARE TINY HOUSES? TYPES OF TINY

HOUSES..................................................28

CHAPTER 5: TIPS AND TRICKS OF LIVING IN A TINY HOUSE

........................................................36

CHAPTER 6: IS TINY HOUSE LIVING FOR YOU?................49

CHAPTER 7: USING SPACE EFFICIENTLY...........................54

CHAPTER 8: THE ECO-FRIENDLY BENEFITS ......................62

CHAPTER 9: ORGANIZATIONAL HOW-TO'S—MAXIMIZE

THAT TINY SPACE!........................................79

CHAPTER 10: A DETAILED PROCESS OF HOW TO PUT UP
YOUR TINY HOUSE ........................................................ 84

CHAPTER 11: SMALL HOUSE FURNISHING ..................... 102

CHAPTER 12: BUILDING THE RIGHT MENTALITY FOR TINY
HOUSE LIVING ............................................................. 116

CHAPTER 13: DESIGN IDEAS AND TIPS........................... 122

CHAPTER 14: UTILITIES AND APPLIANCES...................... 129

CHAPTER 15: PRINCIPLES AND STEPS BEHIND A
SUCCESSFUL MINIMALIST LIFE....................................... 136

CHAPTER 16: HOW TO BEGIN LIVING IN A TINY HOUSE?153

CHAPTER 17: DECLUTTERING AND GUILT ...................... 160

CHAPTER 18: BUILDING A FOUNDATION ....................... 166

CONCLUSION................................................................ 186

# Introduction

A social movement called "Tiny Living" has swept across the globe, creating an interest among people who are looking at rightsizing their lifestyles. The movement encourages folks to look closely at how they are currently living and make a dramatic change.

At the center of this movement is downsizing residential spaces by moving from traditional houses to tiny homes. Other elements of tiny living include self-sufficiency, creating sound fiscal plans, life simplification, and environmental consciousness.

The average American family size has remained the same throughout the decades. However, the space needed to live comfortably has considerably increased. This has made a huge impact on the economy as most of these houses were bought on loans.

There are also environmental concerns associated with living luxuriously big. There is more demand for energy and the carbon footprint left behind has become catastrophic.

This book contains information that will help you evaluate whether living in a tiny house is a change which will work for you. The following topics are included:

• What is a Tiny House?

- The History of the Tiny House or Tiny Living Movement

- Why Move to a Tiny House?

- The Benefits of Living in a Tiny House

- Things to Think Through before Making the Move

- Top 10 Considerations for a Move to a Tiny House

- Adjusting to Your Tiny House

# Chapter 1: The blueprint

Whether you intend to build in the back yard or use a trailer to make into your tiny home, you must have some idea of the square footage that you have available for conversion into living space. There are several obvious elements that will need to be incorporated and these include:

Kitchen space

Sleeping space

Toiletry space

Living space

Add to that the fact that the home will also need storage space and the availability of electricity and water supply and you have quite a complex outline of what the home needs to incorporate. In traditional buildings, there will also be the need for insulation and this is even more important if you intend to take your small home onto the road. Weather conditions will affect how livable that home will be and the difference in temperature between the outdoors and the indoors needs to be taken into account at the blueprint stage. Don't worry, even the DIY enthusiast with no experience can manage all of these elements.

Since every bit of available space is needed to make the most of the small home, plans should be drawn up that include all of the elements that are important to your lifestyle. In this image, you can see that a bed area has been placed above the normal living space, but that the *stairs have been cleverly incorporated to include cupboards*. The kitchen space is minimal and the ceilings have been left high, to create the impression of space.

Thus, the most important part of the construction of a small home is the plan or blueprint and when drawing this out, you don't have to be a professional. You just need to be aware that size matters and that the size of the items incorporated into the house will determine movement space and space to live your everyday life.

The blueprint should also have the exact measurements of the space so that you are able to plan effectively what you can include within the home. The blueprint that you *design for your small house project can be in simple line drawings* or drawn three dimensionally to give you a better idea of the working layout.

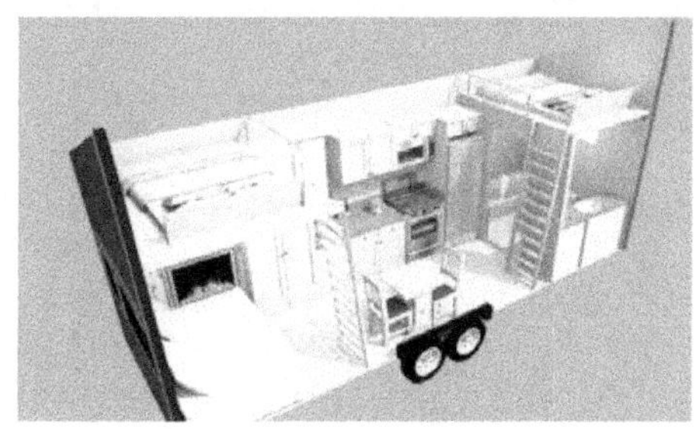

In this trailer for example, the homeowner has the benefit of portability, as well as function, with ample space for two beds and a third when the seating area is folded down.

What the planning stage should also take into account is how to use outside space as this becomes exceptionally important. As you begin to read about the small home lifestyle, you will also understand the significance of this aspect being included in your planning. Think of your blueprint, in a case such as a tiny house, as your way of putting together a lifestyle within a small space. The elements that are important to you need to be available and it is possible that multi-function areas will help you to achieve this. For example, the kitchen area could be covered when not in use, so as to free up space for creating a worktop for your home office.

## Chapter 2: Converted Homes

Although standard housing is widely available for all citizens, there are home owners who prefer a more unconventional setup. After all, a 2,622 square feet land area may have too much of a wasted space for a household who has no need for it. Instead of buying ordinary houses, many Americans and even people elsewhere on the globe have turned to "converted homes". To a keenly practical individual, any building or huge object that has outlived its true purpose can be transformed into a shelter with livable interior space. These are the varieties of tiny (small) converted homes that are relatively well-known today:

Shipping Containers

According to a number of online sources, there are over 17 million shipping containers that are circulated globally. Only a quarter of this roughly estimated inventory are actively used for transport, while approximately 675 of these are lost at sea each year. These are the facts gathered as recently as year 2014. If not for the ingenious individual that has thought of another better use for inactive shipping containers, the world might possibly feel sorry for the three-fourths of those idle vessels being tirelessly manufactured in China (as well as over 600 of them drowning at sea each year). However, the history of shipping container homes is a relatively sketchy Not everyone knew when it exactly began despite the fact that using these huge trade chests for shelter has become globally widespread and prevalent.

The earliest record for using shipping containers as shelters dates back as 1965. Insbrandtsen Company Incorporated filed a patent titled *Combination shipping container and showcase.* The main idea is to use shipping containers as mobile exhibition booth during commercial fairs. However, the idea of using shipping containers as a home only came around half a decade later as a brainchild of a British architect named Nicholas Lacey. In the 1970's, he submitted a university thesis that advocates reusing shipping containers as alternative habitable dwelling. After about ten years, an American architect named Phillip Clark fine-tuned Lacey's ideas and provided a feasible blueprint for an economical converted home. The Patent 4854094, also known as the *Method for converting one or more shipping containers into habitable building*, was officially granted in 1987. It became the earliest standard for converting shipping containers into a cost-efficient and durable home.

An ordinary shipping container has a standard dimension of 20 feet in length and 8 feet in width. This hardly ever scratches the 400 square feet limit of the small house. Thus, a shipping container often serves as a perfect model for a tiny (micro) home due to its relative limited space. However, the often impractical restrictions of a single shipping container allows builders to combine at least two in order to build a more livable interior room. As a habitable dwelling, it has its own advantages and shortcomings.

One of the key advantages of opting for shipping container homes is the relative cost efficiency factor. Compared to purchasing a standard house in a suburban zone, buying and renovating a shipping container is significantly cheaper. A resident can definitely do away with the steep periodic mortgage fees for both the house and lot. Although renting an apartment is seemingly less costly, apartment units cannot be owned. The long-term cost calculation (let's say, after twenty years) is actually horrific in comparison to something which can be possessed in a single or limited transaction.

Another benefit of living in shipping containers is that it is both eco-friendly and industrially resourceful. In United States and all other commercially competitive nations, the wholesale purchase of shipping containers barely cover the number of its actual usage. Converting them into homes solves the problem of shipping container abandonment. Unlike conventional houses, one can save natural resources required in producing shipping container homes.

Lastly, shipping containers are manufactured for its durability. With its capacity to withstand relative kinetic pressure, these homes provide an ideal protection from weathering. Shipping container homes are more stable and durable in terms of having a multi-storied layout compared to conventional structures.

While its benefits are noteworthy, it is also important to consider its relative disadvantages. For one thing, a shipping container is composed solely of steel. This makes temperature control a very problematic issue for home owners. A significant amount of time and resources are often devoted to maintaining the ideal climate inside this type of converted home. If not the temperature, home owners who bought a much cheaper substandard variety will have to bear with the rust, which prompts many to invest largely on its interior renovation. Lastly, shipping containers were not originally designed for long-term habitation. The vapors from the chemical components used in manufacturing a shipping container is harmful for the health.

It is also very important to keep in mind that some of the shipping containers were already used and the spillages and residue chemicals left after its commercial transit might still be harmful. Buying a shipping container for a small house is a huge bargain, yet significant costs in restoration and face-lift are required to create a pleasant and livable interiors.

Army Huts

Necessity is the mother of all invention. And as history proves it, no other man-made event can impel so much urgency than war. For all its dreadfulness, war has oftentimes revolutionized the way humanity has lived. It updated the quality of medical services more efficiently. War also allowed engineers to design more advanced means of transportation. In the particular case of revolutionizing shelters, even war has contributed its own brand of utilitarian ingenuity.

During World War I, the allied nations of France and United Kingdom was at war with Germany. When one of the many French villages felt the onslaught of bombing by the German artillery, England has sent one of its best natural engineers to provide support. Lieutenant Colonel Peter Nissen designed a shelter that is strong, yet simple and very easy to build. The Nissen Huts became the first model for the semi-cylindrical cross-section army shelter used by the military from World War I up to the contemporary times. It was said that Nissen Huts are so easy to build that it only takes an average of about 4 hours for six people to complete, while all the materials needed can fit in a single 3-ton truck. This revolutionary design earned Nissen an equivalent of US $19,000 (a significant sum in that era).

During World War II, the Nissen Huts have come to the attention of the allied United States navy engineers. They retained the original design from their British allies yet they aimed to fabricate something much bigger and more durable. The Quonset Huts were then first manufactured in the namesake region of Quonset Point in Rhode Island. Unlike the Nissen Huts predecessor, Quonset Huts were not only limited to its use as a sleeping quarters. It has become any functional building for the United States armed forces such as mess halls, bars, offices and even an armory. Approximately 153,000 Quonset huts were manufactured by the United States navy.

By the end of the war, the United States economy is on its way to steady growth and expansion. However, there was a particular problem in terms of housing the returning military servicemen. There were not enough homes available and the current pace of real estate development at the time cannot catch up to the sheer demand. As a result, discharged military engineers began converting the surplus Quonset Huts to shelter the returning homeless veterans. It was a best solution at the time since each surplus shelters were sold at bottom $2700 price (since the process of dismantling and recycling is more costly and labor intensive). It also made the transition to civilian life much easier. This positive feedback has allowed the US Public Housing Authority to develop several subdivisions of Quonset Huts at the outskirts of the urban centers.

The Nissen and Quonset Huts have their peculiar shape as an advantage. The arching hull provides excellent structural stability and aerodynamic buffer. Since these army huts are largely made of galvanized steel, these houses can withstand a considerable measure of physical impact (exactly the way the military designed it to sustain itself in overall combat scenario). Lastly, these army huts also prove to be weather-tight, providing good insulation for the interiors and preventing leakage that is practically unavoidable in conventional buildings.

The original Quonset Huts may not pass as a tiny house due to its standard 720 square feet area. However, sizes have become customizable since its introduction to the civilian world. These army huts are among the most durable and reliable converted homes ever produced in the 21$^{st}$ Century. They have been steadily mass produced and distributed for over 60 years.

# Chapter 3: What are tiny houses?

What are tiny houses and why do they seem to be so popular nowadays?

By definition, tiny houses are houses that do not exceed 400 square feet in terms of livable space.

This is very small when compared to a typical American home which is upwards of 2,600 square feet at the very minimum.

This recent shift in housing preference has taken the world by storm. Nowadays you have tiny houses, tiny communities, tiny living and other space minimizing ideas and there doesn't seem to be any end to this "trend".

Who can benefit from tiny houses?

Anyone can benefit from building a tiny house. You can be a young professional who is constantly on the move or a pensioner who wants to see more of the world. The beauty of having a tiny house is that you can bring it along with you so you won't have any issues when it comes to housing.

Aside from that, the entire world also benefits from tiny houses. Since tiny houses consume very little of the Earth's resources, you can effectively minimize your carbon footprint.

How much does a tiny house cost?

A tiny house is approximately a fifth of the size of a conventional home. This means you will need lesser materials to build it. Therefore, a tiny house can be considered relatively cheap to build. This is the perfect solution for young people who are just starting out or individuals who want to own a home but do not have access to sizeable house loans.

A normal tiny house is just around $20,000 to $40,000. If you decide to build it on your own, you can even bring that sticker price further down. Owning a home for the price of a mid-level car is actually a fair deal if you think about it.

If you do take out a loan in order to build your tiny house, you'll be able to pay it off in a shorter amount of time. This will then allow you to free up your resources for other things.

Building and owning a tiny house not only frees you from the soaring prices of housing, it also has the potential of freeing you from the constraints of what normal society deems as acceptable. You can devote your energy to pursuing what you are passionate about. You can also free yourself from accumulating unnecessary stuff. And last but not the least, owning a tiny house has the potential of giving you real freedom.

# Chapter 4: What are tiny houses?
## Types of Tiny Houses.

With tiny homes popping up all across the country, not many seem surprised to hear someone speak of their desire to "go small." Everyone seems to be on overdrive to save money, reduce carbon footprints, and see what it feels like to live with less.

However, it is easier said than done to buy or build such a small accommodation. A large number of things need to be considered such as the lifestyle of the inmates and the actual construction to be followed. Moreover, this is a national movement not everyone can participate in.

Here are ten questions that every home owner must ask before deciding whether and how to buy a tiny house:

- There will be a sizable cost to pay upfront so do you have enough money to spare?

- Building a smaller home can be a major challenge. Are you up for it?

- Construction of a tiny property can take as long as a year or two so are you willing to wait?

- Picture a one-car garage. Will you be able to live in a space smaller than that?

- Is it okay if you are forced to live with just one pair of shoes?

- Do you have the space where you can park it? A driveway will do but you still need to own one!

- Splitting resources is the best way you can live in a tiny house. Are you willing to share?

- Some tiny homes come with bathrooms and others don't. Will you be comfortable answering Nature's call in unconventional ways?

- Is your lifestyle suited to the limitations of living in a tiny house?

- Does your home mean more than just four walls and a roof?

Tiny homes are available in a variety of types, but they tend to fit into two categories: moveable and non-moveable.

A moveable tiny house is on some sort of wheels, while a non-moveable home is built on a foundation.

Traveling Tiny Homes

There are technically three types of tiny homes that you can travel in. Only one of these is considered a "true" tiny home based on the exterior and interior combined. You should also be aware that all three options would be considered RV living.

Trailer Tiny Home

This is the traditional tiny home that has become the "fad" of the new millennium. This style tiny house is built with wood or metal framing, regular home siding, shingled or metal roof, and outfitted inside just the house you desire it to be. You start from scratch and create a structure that is architecturally impressive, but also fits on a trailer of up to 65 feet, max, including the towing vehicle.

Converted Bus

School buses and other commercial buses have been used to convert them into a tiny house, for affordable living. There are buses that can be purchased already set up for RV style living. Music groups often travel in buses, but these are highly expensive. There have been some individuals who have bought old transportation buses, removed the seats, windows, and created their tiny home inside. They have made it look like a real house indoors versus the RV style of most travel buses.

RVs

RVs such as motorhomes are still tiny houses. They are just made for camping versus a consistent home. It is not that you can't live in a motorhome, permanently. Many have for decades as part of circuses, fairs, and festivals. However, they are outfitted more for camping, with camping style beds, bathrooms, and kitchens. It is also possible to buy an old RV, remove the interior and set it up like a tiny home with granite countertops, more vertical wall space, and better storage concepts.

Non-Moveable Tiny Houses

Any architect can design you a house that is smaller than the typical home. It will be built on a foundation, and be to your specifications. However, there is one more option besides the typical wood frame house that you can choose as a non-moveable home.

 You can go with a "container" home. You can pick up shipping containers anywhere from $1,000 to $6,000. You can then have doors and windows cut into the steel, have frames welded in place for the doors and windows, and modify the interior of one or more containers to create your tiny home. The movement is extremely popular in coastal cities with shipyards. It is possible to pick up one-use containers, meaning they have only traveled on the sea one way or for a round trip.

Container homes are also popular in hurricane states. The heavy steel of the containers makes it difficult for the home to be damaged in a hurricane, particularly, if the steel doors are left on to cover the main entrance into the home.

# Chapter 5: Tips and Tricks of Living in a Tiny House

Now that you have an idea about how to go forth with this, you definitely should begin to "try" how tiny houses work, just to get a gist of how they work, and to see if you—and your family—could adjust to it. For this, you have to be mindful of the following:

Consider your way of life, together with your family size. Are there children who still need to go to school? Do you often invite friends over, or hold extravagant parties? Do you think you will be able to make the switch without having so much of a hard time?

Try some excursion lodges. Lease at least one of them—they'd give you the feel of what a tiny house is. Once you're there, you can begin to weigh the pros and cons of tiny house living. You will begin to understand how it is to move with only little space available, and see if you actually like it, or if it is not for you. This way, you won't waste time moving if you don't think it will actually fit in your life, and make you feel good at all.

Make sure that there's a lot of open air, and open spaces. Even if you decide to live in a tiny house, you'd have to make sure that plenty of air would still be able to go around, and that you would not be suffocated in any way. You can then look for homes located in entryway patios, or those with land masses and substantial decks around.

Make way for utilities. The thing about tiny houses is that there should be easy ways of getting access to utilities such as running water, power, or sewage. You need to have these things integrated with your house. Ask yourself how you'll be able to have internet access, and if you can make use of oriental water boards. You have to learn how to survey your grounds, and see what you can make use of—and what could work for you.

Make sure that you adhere to zoning/construction standards. It would be such a waste to put up a house and then end up having it deconstructed just because you have not checked for construction or zoning laws. No matter how small your home is, there are still rules that have to be followed—make sure that you are aware of them.

Have less. Clean up the clutter in your house, and decide what needs to be thrown away. If you feel like there are certain things others can use, give or sell them away. Throw things you have not used in months—you can always make do with just a few clothes around. Don't let the thought of being overly "sentimental" turn you into such a hoarder. A small home would definitely feel big without all the excess clutter in your life.

Do Less. It's not about being lazy, or about being such a procrastinator. Mostly, this has to do with being able to do a lot in just a short period of time. Quality over quantity, as they say. Curtail your to-do list, your workload, and your duties. Curtail the amount of events in your calendar—do you really have to attend that family reunion every week? Do you have to attend that certain party each Friday night? It is about learning what your priorities are, and deciding to focus on them instead of the unnecessary things in life. Do it gradually, and you'll see the positive effects for yourself.

Create Less. Improve the state of your life, and what you already have instead of focusing on creating things that you have no idea would work. Focus on what you already have, appreciate them, and maximize their use. Don't be someone who creates unnecessary noise, and unnecessary drama in life—you will only stress yourself out that way. Focus on your work, and give your best in what you have to do—the rest will soon follow.

Don't waste too much time online. Unless your work is online, remember that you have the right to decide to stay away from using social media too much. Sometimes, the things you see online could dictate your mood, and affect how you feel—and when you get overly stressed, it could be quite toxic for you. Try to do other things: journal, instead of blog, go out, watch TV, watch movies, read books—just give yourself some time to live in the real world—and not the virtual world all the time.

Consume less! Don't feel like you need to have everything just to feel good in this world. When you have what you already need, you would feel happier if you just begin to appreciate them, instead of focusing on what you think you lack. Do not magnify what you don't have and you will feel so much better.

Don't forget to think about the location

The location of your tiny house should also be one of your priorities. Again, zoning restrictions should be kept in mind, but aside from that, you also have to be mindful of the following:

Fabricated Homes

If you have a fabricated home—or one that is rooted in one location, you may try the following locations:

Wee Casa—Colorado. Currently, there are ten lots here that are available for rental, but only for short term living purposes. This means you would have to move somewhere else in 3 to 6 months.

Portland Garden Cottages—Oregon. You can rent a lot here for a minimum of a month. However, you have to make calls right away because there are only very few lots available, and they are meant for smaller tiny houses that are at most 364 square feet.

Getaway House--New Hampshire. Aside from lot rentals, you can make use of community getaway provisions (i.e., meals, snacks, activities), as well as composting toilets and showers—so you can opt not to install those in your house.

Dignity Village—Oregon. If you have limited income, you can try looking for parking space at Dignity Village in Oregon as affordably-priced rentals are around for the whole year. Currently, they are supporting around 60 residents.

Blue Moon Rising—Maryland. This eco-friendly tourist retreat offers rentals for land that are 275 to 400 square feet, or tiny houses that can accommodate up to 4 people.

RV Parks

Of course, you can also try RV Parks—or places where you can park your RV tiny house at. These could be any of the following:

Pine Acres Campground—South Carolina. This is located at 205 Duke Drive, Aiken, South Carolina. You have to make sure, though that your tiny house only has 30/50 amp power to be able to rent a patch of land here.

Oceanside Beachfront RV Resort—Oregon. This provides a tranquil setting for tiny house owners everywhere. To make rentals and reservations, visit the park at 90281 Cape Arago Highway, Coos Bay, Oregon.

Hidden Acres Family Campground—Virginia. Another easy place to stay in! You can visit it at 17391 Richard Turnpike, Milford, Bowling Green, Virginia.

Evergreen RV Park--California. This is located at 2135 N Oxnard Boulevard in Oxnard, California. The park accepts tiny homes that are RVIA certified—or those with certification from the Recreation Vehicle Industry Association.

Creekside RV Park and Cain Plantation—Georgia. This is probably one of the most hassle-free parks to park in as it requires no notices or RVIA certifications. This is located at 6143 U.S. Highway 41 North, Hahira, Georgia.

Creek N Wood Campground—New York. This is another easy place to stay in—no certification or notices needed! You can visit the place at 2528 Wheeler Station Road, East Bloomfield, New York.

Cloudbase RV Park—Tennessee. This is one of the most popular RV Parks in the United States. The only problem is that it is almost always full, so make sure that you visit and make a reservation first. You can find it just at the south of Chattanooga, near Wildwood, Georgia.

Christmas RV Park—Florida. Nope, this isn't just open on Christmas; it is open every day of the year—just make sure that your tiny house is RVIA certified. You can visit this RV Park at 25525 E. Colonial Drive, Christmas, Florida.

All Seasons RV Park—California. Located at Interstate 15 Exit 41, this also accepts tiny homes that are certified by the RVIA. You also should give them a month's notice before parking your tiny house there.

If you're quite the minimalist or you know you want to move around a lot, it might be best for you to just rent space for your tiny house. You can start with the aforementioned examples, or look for one near your place.

# CHAPTER 6: IS TINY HOUSE LIVING FOR YOU?

Interest in Tiny House living has been spawned by TV shows such as Tiny House Nation and Tiny House Hunters. However, the average person is probably little more than a voyeur when it comes to tiny houses, looking on with curiosity and wondering about the lifestyle of those who have actually taken this plunge. Tiny house living is not for everyone!

THE CHALLENGES OF LIVING IN A TINY HOUSE

People who have opted to live in a tiny house can usually cite good solid reasons to back up the commitment that which choices like this requires. For most, the financial freedom which comes with this lifestyle is a driving force. Zero debt and no longer being married to a lifestyle which is all consuming has a great appeal. It may mean no longer having to work hard at an unfulfilling job in favor of spending time with family, and the ability to pursue rewarding activities. Some people simply don't want to be tied down – they like to travel and prefer to live in a place that they can easily leave – or take with them! Most tiny house dwellers are also pleased to have a healthy relationship with the environment – some of them envision themselves working towards a totally sustainable, self-sufficient existence.

That said, the decision to live in a small house is life-altering and there are some challenges in the day to day which may be unforeseen.

Living in a small space means having to keep it tidy – everything is in plain view and space is at a premium. Where you eat may be the same place where you are going to be sitting next to work at your laptop. A messy space can be anxiety provoking when you can't close a door on it!

When you live in a tiny house, you cannot realistically entertain or indulge space consuming hobbies like you used to.

Less storage means that you will probably be spending more time cooking and preparing foods. You will also need to be more organized and plan ahead. On the upside, you will probably be eating fresher foods.

If you don't live alone, you will be spending more time connected to those you live with - in close quarters. Everyone appreciates and needs time alone - you'll have to work hard to find a way to make this happen in a Tiny House. The upside – most people find themselves extending their space to the great outdoors.

If you are committed to the idea of Tiny House living, you will have to become creative in the way you deal with these types of practical issues and will more than likely draw on resources you never realized you had.  Bear in mind - necessity

is the mother of invention!

# Chapter 7: Using Space Efficiently

One thing you'll have to seriously consider, if you intend to live in a tiny house, is how to use the available space you have as efficiently as possible.

Three things that you definitely should have in your tiny house include a sleeping area, a toilet and bath and a kitchen. There's no way around this and you definitely should have these spaces in your tiny house at whatever cost possible.

How much space do you really need to comfortably use your toilet and bath? Measure your body dimensions and triple this and you can have one that has all the necessary amenities like a composting toilet (if you don't go for the flush type toilet) and room to move around as you take your showers.

What about your kitchen? How much space do you really need? How many appliances do you actually own and do you really need that much to live comfortably. For most people, a kitchen equipped with a refrigerator, a stove and a sink is enough. Making everything fit without taking away a lot of the precious real estate is going to be a definite challenge but it is possible as most tiny house owners have shown throughout the years.

You can opt for smaller appliances, you can have a sink big enough to wash everything as comfortably as possible and you can have either a full stove or a tabletop one that you can easily stow away when not in use. Scour the internet and your local camping and outdoor stores for appliances that have been miniaturized to fit in RVs and camping bags. These are the items that you can put in your own home and comfortably use without sacrificing too much space.

Last but not the least, your sleeping area. Most people who live in tiny houses opt to have a loft type of bedroom that they can climb up to when it's time to sleep. This is where the saying: "if it's not broken, don't fix it" comes into play. Since it seems to work for most people, try considering a loft type of bedroom as your sleeping area. This may prove challenging to some people but over time, if you get used to it, it will become easier in the long run.

If it's any consolation, climbing up and down to your sleeping area should give you a little bit of exercise early in the morning and at night, which can result to more physical fitness in the end.

So, define where these three areas are going to go first then design the rest of the house as you see fit.

One way to make your tiny house seem bigger is to allow the outdoors to come in. You can do this by installing huge windows, allowing more light into the house in the process. You can also install huge bay doors that open up or slide away to open up your house some more. This will take some serious funding but the benefits you can derive from having all that open space are priceless.

One positive side effect people who live in tiny houses experience is that the more they live in such a confined space, the more they become aware of their carbon footprint. Minimalism and mindfulness is also enhanced. You can't have too many stuff in your tiny house or else, you'll have so much clutter and little to no space to comfortably move in much less, live in.

Here are some more practical solutions to using space efficiently in your tiny house:

Shelves and cupboards

Installing shelves in your tiny house can increase the storage space for your items.

You can also install additional cupboards so you can effectively keep most of your belongings away and out of sight to reduce that cluttered look.

Sliding doors

Swinging doors take up a lot of space when opened, which can lead to a temporary blockage every time you use them. To get around this, you may want to employ sliding doors. These take up a lesser space than a conventional door and can add a little more character to your tiny house.

Multiple function furniture/ concealable furniture

Multiple function furniture items have become all the craze right now for a lot of tiny house and RV owners, as they can maximize the limited space they have in their dwellings and have multiple functions for items that take a lot of space when they are not in use. Having the ability to fold or conceal them in any possible means also increases your living space when they are not in use so make sure to look into this.

In conclusion, increasing your space inside your tiny house can best be left to just how imaginative you can be. After setting your mind to it, you can actually come up with a lot of good ideas and perhaps, innovate existing methods. If you do have a very unique idea, you may even want to share it with the rest of the tiny house community and you can be sure it will help a whole lot of people scratching their heads right now who are looking for some space saving solutions.

# Chapter 8: The Eco-Friendly Benefits

Tiny Homes might be small, but their advantages are enormous! For many people, living in a Tiny Home means financial well-being; for others, it means they have the freedom to be mobile and live where they want when they want. Then, there are those people whose concerns are for the planet as much as for their wallet. You don't need to be a '70s hippie or a tree-hugger to understand that people are consuming far more of the earth's resources than can be replaced. When we see clear evidence of global warming, the erosion of our ozone, and the sad extinction of our wildlife, it's no wonder those concerned about the planet are turning to Tiny Homes. It's quite eye opening how much each Tiny Home saves and protects our earth.

If you're entertaining the wisdom of investing in a Tiny Home, maybe the following facts will help you hurdle some of your obstacles and give it a try. Not only do Tiny Homes tear down personal living costs, but they also significantly reduce the impact that construction waste, lumber squandering, and the over-the-top emission of CO2 into our atmosphere. Let's break this down a bit further, shall we?

Tiny Homes Minimize Construction Waste

Approximately 40% of our planet's solid waste, in one way or another, is generated by construction. It's jaw-dropping how much of a difference in waste occurs when building a Tiny Home of about 200–300 square feet to that of a regular home of around 2,600 square feet. Between framing, tiling, sheathing, roofing, siding, and concrete, a close approximation of waste for a Tiny Home is 400 pounds, while you can expect to haul about 5,000 USD of waste from a regular-sized home. Even Tiny Home Builders who aren't being particularly conscious of using reclaimed materials experience these differences first-hand. The Tiny Home dweller can provide evidence showing just a simple build has a big difference due to home size alone.

Timber Usage Minimized in a Tiny Home

In the United States, almost three-quarters of the entire consumption of timber each year is from the private housing industry. While it's admirable to recycle paper products, it can't begin to make the dent in timber usage that building a Tiny Home can. It takes more than 90% more wood to build a 2,600-square foot home than it does to build a 200-square foot Tiny Home. Using less timber means less power to cut, age, split, finish, store, and haul. What could be hauled in a few hours to build a Tiny Home might take repeated trips over several days to drag on the building site of a regular-sized home. Therefore, building Tiny Homes also saves on diesel gas as well as fossil fuel.

Comparing the Emissions of CO2

The release of CO2 into the earth's atmosphere has played havoc with our global climate, and it is considered the most active participants in the creation of global warming. Although some politicians would like to pretend that global warming doesn't exist, science paints an entirely different picture of its effects. Global warming has caused our ice caps to recede and our seas to rise. Our wildlife habitats have been devastated by global warming, causing over a million-different species to become extinct and bringing others to the brink of extinction.

Almost 18% of the earth's greenhouse gasses are emitted from the private housing industry at an astronomical rate. A 3,000-square foot house will emit 28,000 pounds of CO2 per year into the earth's atmosphere, as opposed to only 2,000 pounds of CO2 per year from a Tiny Home. While being elegantly small, Tiny Homes are incredibly efficient, using only 914 kWh of electricity per year compared to 12,773 kWh per year in a regular-sized build. It doesn't take rocket science to figure out that the savings in electricity, heating, and cooling of your Tiny Home is going to be positively reflected in your monthly finances as well.

Eco-Friendly Devices and Practices

There are things Tiny Home dwellers regularly do that allows them to be totally "off the grid" and live in harmony with their environment. Most of the time, these aren't extraordinary measures taken by Tiny Homeowners, but rather, it is the norm for them. We have listed some of these eco-friendly devices and practices so that you can get an idea of the Tiny Home lifestyle.

Composting Toilet

A compost toilet is a waterless system that uses an aerobic process to decompose human excrement. The best composting toilets divert the urine from the solids and then use a fan run by a generator to dry the solid waste further. If the bathroom works well and the device is proper, there will be no odor, and the waste can be used to fertilize a garden or plants. Depending on how many people are living in your Tiny Home, the toilet will need to be emptied and cleaned out about every 3 to 4 weeks.

Although composting toilets will save you about $50 a month on your water bill if you are hooked up to city services, the initial cost of a compost toilet can be much more expensive.  While the expense of a flushing toilet is a price of $100 to $200, a composting toilet will cost about $1,500 to $4,000.  This device is not done to save the Tiny Home dweller money, but to allow them to be self-sustainable and not depend on public services.

Before you decide on a composting toilet, if you are living in the city, be sure to check with city codes—some prohibit their use within the city limits.  If a composting toilet is your choice, you can also dilute the urine and turn it into the gray water for use in the garden.  Dried solid waste can be utilized for that purpose as well.

Solar and Wind Power

Using the earth as a resource to power your Tiny Home is commonly achieved, but don't think it's going to cost you next to nothing. It's initially much more expensive to construct your Tiny Home using eco-friendly devices, but there's a beauty in doing so. You can live in the middle of nowhere, entirely independent of any outside services and their costs. Throughout the years, these eco-friendly devices will pay for themselves, and allow you the freedom that few have; however, if you are working on a limited budget, it might take a while to purchase and implement these systems.

Solar cells and the wind can totally power a Tiny Home. You'll first need to decide the size of your Tiny Home and how many people will be living in it. Then, you'll need to determine what will be run from your Tiny Home. For instance, will your stove be gas or electric? How much water will you need to heat in an average day? Will the area where you'll be living provide sufficient sun rays and wind? If not, how big a generator will you need? There are lots of questions to be answered, and the answers vary on your private use of the Tiny Home.

You might need a solar calculator to determine the number of solar panels needed to provide power. Once you have calculated the number of solar cells, then decide whether you can install them on the roof of your home or you'll need some free-standing panels. Wherever you place your solar panels, be sure to keep them out of the way of trees or shrubs that might block the sun or damage them. Depending on your needs, wind power can be accomplished by installing a rooftop wind turbine.

The following is a creative design that shows built-in solar cells that coat the rooftop and a wind turbine attached to the capsule. Although this is an ultra-modern design currently being used more for research and commercial office space in remote areas, it just might be the wave of the future for Tiny Home dwellers.

Gray Water and Rain Water Harvesting System

Most areas are not going to have enough rainfall to provide all the water you'll need each month, but a substantial amount can be harvested before having to tap into your backup supply.  If your Tiny Home is going to be stationary, then you might want to consider a sizeable cistern to store rainwater.  The average water needs are as follows.

Drinking Water Per Person1 Gallon

Toilet (if flushable)2 Gallons Per Flush

Shower2 Gallons Per Minute

Of course, this does not include the water needed for cooking or washing your hands, dishes, and clothing.  If we assume the average conservative adult will use 15 gallons of water a day, that would require approximately four inches of rainfall a month. Naturally, the water needs will increase for each additional person living in the Tiny Home. In most locations, rain doesn't fall each day or month equally, so it is necessary to have a storage device. One such device is a rain pillow.

This one is large and can be stored outside, if weather permits, but you can also get them in all sizes to conveniently fit beneath a bed or under a cabinet as well. Since they are inflatable, they are easy to empty and store when you are on the move.

Propane Power

Propane tanks are easy to install in a Tiny Home.  One of the things to be aware of is that warm-climate propane is different than the cold-climate one.  The butane levels are higher in cold-climates.  It's a good practice to always use the propane in the area to which you purchased it.  If not, trade in your tanks and buy new when you relocate.  The propane is usually attached outside on the trailer or the side of a stationary Tiny Home.

Propane will supply power to things like a gas stove and electricity, should your solar and wind power not be adequate, to heat your water. It can also run your air conditioning and heating as well.

Building Green

During the building process, you'll want to make use of all the repurposed and reclaimed supplies possible. For insulation, wood construction, and storage space within your Tiny Home, using reclaimed and repurposed materials will help you do your part to protect the planet. Because your needs will be smaller in size, much of your building supplies can be obtained from other larger-sized building sites. Visit your local builder and ask if you can salvage scrap from their builds. Most will be happy to help and appreciate the time and money saved to haul their wasted building products to a construction dump. (BUT DO NOT STEAL MATERIALS)

These are just a few of the items to consider if your desire is to live off the grid or to go green as much as possible. Although it's much easier to install these products during your build, if a limited budget holds you back, you can always do a little at a time. Every little bit counts in resources consumed and money saved.

# Chapter 9: Organizational How-To's—Maximize That Tiny Space!

As we already know, a tiny house doesn't really have as big a storage space as one might hope. The closet space will be very limited, as well as the kitchen cabinets and pantry. This is why it is very important to be innovative in organizing your things. Remember that a tiny space as little as 400 square feet will not hide any signs of your untidiness. Good thing there are tiny tricks that will help you big time to maximize all you have in a tiny space.

Dead and vertical spaces

Exploit as many dead and vertical spaces as you possibly can. While still undergoing construction, have custom-built furniture that has hidden storage space underneath. This is particularly applicable to couches and beds where the space below is usually not utilized. There are ottomans with hollow centers and removable seats that you can use to store small things. You can also make the staircase a closet space by taking advantage of all the vertical space under it. Installing cabbies above the windows will be another way to make use of a space that would otherwise be vacant and wasted.

Murphy bed and loft

Both a murphy bed and a loft offer space-saving options. A murphy bed will allow you to have extra space to do other activities during the day when you don't need the bed and it is stored away. Meanwhile, a loft will enable you to use the vertical space above the other rooms in your tiny house.

Lazy Susan

Just when you think a corner cabinet is such an inefficient use or big waste of space, the lazy Susan will make you think otherwise. Having that mechanism on the corner of a kitchen cabinet does not only make the space more useful but also very accessible. Now you can store pots, pans, and spice jars in that used-to-be-hard-to-reach area.

**Magnets**

This smart storage idea is turning into a rage in the tiny house movement. And why wouldn't it be? It's not only innovative—it can also be incorporated into the overall design aspect of the house. By permanently installing magnets on the walls, the ceiling and/or under hanging kitchen cabinets and using jars that are made of metal or have metal lids, the dead space will now have a purpose. You can also use the magnet to hang kitchen equipment like pots, pans and knives (be cautious though!) and other things in your home.

Keep everything tidy!

No matter what your innovative idea of creating a storage space might be, if you don't keep your things clean and in order, then these innovative ideas of yours will not be of use at all. Like what I have said many times before, tiny houses are not for the messy, untidy people. Just a few items that are not in their proper places will definitely make your tiny house cluttered and crammed.

# Chapter 10: **A Detailed Process of How to Put Up Your Tiny House**

Here's the thing: Not everyone can own a patch of land and decide to park his tiny house there. In that case, you may decide to rent land instead. According to most tiny house land renters, this is basically what it costs them in a month:

*$125/month*. If you can find land that you can rent, you can pay just around $125 in a month. In some cases, you can rent for free during the summer, which saves you $125 in 2 to 3 months. During that time, you can also grow your own vegetables and have some fun out, too.

*Business rental spaces* that allow for tiny houses may cost just around $40/month in some states.

*Property taxes amount to $0.00*—which means you will definitely be able to save a lot of money.

Zoning and Building Codes

Zoning is where it all falls down to.

What you have to understand is that zoning isn't exactly the same as building codes. You have to take note that counties, townships, and cities all have different zoning regulations, and for that you can check out U.S. Zoning Maps to be sure. Zoning is basically about where your tiny house should be located, and what patch of land it can occupy. This involves safety, health, and financial controls. Apart from that, it also includes:

Septic or sewer connections

Emergency vehicle access

Rainway runoff control

Well water or municipal water hookups

Number of residences in a given area

Square feet/lot size

Meanwhile, building codes are about the minimum standards needed for the construction of a house, or the way the house should be built.

So, in summation, Zoning answers where, and building codes answer how a house should be built. In short, you can put up a tiny house as long as it meets building codes and zoning requirements, and as you may have read earlier, there really are areas that are perfect for tiny houses to be parked in.

Building Permits

Now, maybe you're thinking about building permits and whether you need them or not. The answer is that if you are going to build your tiny house in a trailer, it would fall into the category of travel trailer and you can stop thinking about building codes as they would not apply to the said category.

However, for safety measures, it would be best to build your tiny house the same way you would create a real house (re: that it adheres to building codes) so that it would be able to withstand harsh weather conditions.

Now, when your tiny house is determined to fit Shed conditions, you may not have any need for permits. The only problem is that it may not be considered as a good place for dwelling, so you may have to reassess what you have done. Always know your local laws to be sure.

RVIA Certification

As mentioned earlier, if you're going for rentals, you need RVIA Certification. Here are some guidelines:

You should meet ANSI 119.2 (regular RV) or 119.5 (Park RV) standards. In this case, it would be good to consult with designers who can give you free tiny house plans, or get the help of builders who have already created tiny houses before.

If you're looking for RVIA Certification, it would be good to look for a company with the word "Financing" under their name. This way, you might have a chance to get RV Financing which would help ease out your money troubles, if any.

Insurance

You can also check with your insurance agent to know if you can get insurance for your tiny house. It may fall under the category of cabin or travel trailer, which would help you get insurance in the long run.

A Detailed Process

To get permits (if needed), and check if it fits zoning regulations, you should provide officials with a detailed process of how you're going to build your house. This should include the following:

A detailed structural plan that would illustrate where joist, studs, rafters and other engineered materials are located. This should include tension ties, hurricane clips, and the like. You should also explain how secure the house is.

A detailed illustration/explanation of how various parts of the house are connected to the trailer, and how roof, doors, windows, and walls are hinged or sheathed.

Moisture barriers, walls, floors, vapor barriers, and insulators should also be illustrated and explained.

You should provide a detailed diagram of the electrical plan.

You also should provide a complete detailed bill of materials—from where you bought your materials, or if someone donated them. These are important in order to register your house as a tiny house or tiny house on wheels.

Finally, you should provide a statement of your method of construction, as well as names of contractors or sub-contractors that you may have hired.

Meeting Standards

Finally, your tiny house should be able to meet the following standards:

RVIA NFPA 119.2 Standards

You must make sure that the tiny house would keep its residents safe from earthquakes, fires, hurricanes, or other harsh weather conditions. The house should also be able to withstand winds of 130 MPH, and have adequate moisture and vapor barriers, together with fans and insulation.

There should be a secondary means of escape.

You can make way for incinerating or composting toilets, or RV toilets with waste tanks. These break waste down faster, and could be good for the health of residents and neighbors alike.

It should be secured to a trailer that fits with the weight of your house and should weigh less than 10,000 pounds.

You should make use of quality materials, and new structural components, such as plywood, lumber, or steel must meet International Building Code guidelines.

Fasteners should be resistant to corrosion and tie-points should be attached to the foundation or trailer frame.

Use hurricane clips, tension ties, joist hangers and engineered straps that are recommended by most manufacturers.

For enclosed spaces in the house, you have to make sure that they are labeled.

Framing

Welded steel frames must be secured to the trailer.

Wood frames must be able to resist strong winds and rain.

Use only the appropriate headers for doors and windows—it's okay if they're not uniform.

Use hot galvanized ring shank nails for 2 x 4 lumber on frames. Ring screws could be used, too.

Roofs and walls must be sheathed and the use of adhesive fasteners is also recommended for all sheathing.

2 x 4 lumber is good for floors, but you can strengthen them with 2 x 8 lumber.

Use hurricane brackets and threaded rods to tie and secure the walls.

Windows should be laminated and tampered, and roofs should have roof slopes of around 12".

Insulation

Floor and roof insulation should at least be R19.

There must be insulation in between the trailer and the wheel walls, and ½" insulation between floor boards.

Protect indoor air quality with energy recovery ventilators.

Heating Systems

Wood stoves have to be EPA approved and you must also use EPA Piping.

Electric heating systems also have to be UL Approved, and you have to make sure that there is an exterior air inlet under or in the woodstove itself. Make sure that this is completely open.

Try to use 60 cfm ventilation fans, and make sure to turn these off when windows are open to avoid smoking.

Kerosene heaters are not permitted, so avoid them at all costs.

If you're going to use propane heaters, make sure that you have fire/gas alarms ready, just to be on the safe side always.

Electrical, Water, Sewer, Gas Systems

Fasten the pipes in such a way that they would be secured even while moving the house.

Install appliances with extra caulking so that road vibration would be okay.

Make sure all appliances are UL approved, especially those that are installed or attached to the house.

Make use of threaded fittings for gas connections. They should withstand high vibrations, and be extremely flexible.

Fasten heavy objects to the house so moving would not be a problem. These include: bathtubs, wood stoves, propane tanks, water tanks.

Plumbing always has to be vented either to a side wall or on the roof.

Showers, sinks, and toilets also have to be plumbed. Make sure that marine tanks and sanitary sewers could work for easy waste disposal—especially while traveling.

Fire Safety

There should be a smoke detector in the general living area, and also in the bathroom.

A fire extinguisher should always be accessible.

Use a Carbon Monoxide detector if you're using wood stoves, or appliances that emit burning or smoking mechanisms. A Propane-CO Detector is also allowed.

Make sure that there is stable means of going to and from the loft, if said loft is present. This loft could be 5 feet from the main floor or more.

Moving/Parking Guide

Once you're ready to move, make sure that you keep the following tips in mind:

First and foremost, you have to make sure that you know state laws of the state you're moving to, and that there is ample space for tiny houses. You can check Chapter 1 for this.

You may need special permits, depending on the weight, height, and width of your tiny house. You might also need to apply for commercial driver's license. This is because your tiny house might be considered a travel trailer. However, if it's you who's going to drive your own tiny home—and not someone else, you may no longer have to apply for this permit—but again, make sure to check state laws first.

Make sure that weight is properly distributed around the house so you'd be able to easily balance it while traveling. You can purchase and use a trailer tongue weight scale for this.

Make sure that you make a detailed plan of your route before going on the road. This way, you wouldn't have to check a map or GPS which could also be a hassle. It's good to know where you are going right away. This will also help you avoid overpasses and bridges that have low clearances.

Always include the trailer tongue to know how much space you really need for parking. Try to sway it from side to side to get better information.

And, make sure to level the house once you have parked. Use tongue jack for front to back leveling, and Anderson levelers for left to right leveling. Attach two small bubble levels to the house to see if you have leveled properly.

# Chapter 11: Small House Furnishing

Before you move into your tiny home you need to make sure that it is well furnished. This is important as it will help inject life into your small living space. The following are important tips on how to furnish your small house:

**Decoration**

Decorating a tiny house can help you make your house appear bigger and more appealing to you and your visitors. When decorating your small house the best way to make it appear more spacious is to use soft pastel shades in your design. This will help make the house warmer and quite inviting. Also, consider using color to help lift your moods when in your tiny house.

Generally, a small house needs to be fresh and free from clutter. Make use of every available space by building storage cabinets in the walls to ensure that you have enough space to store your belongings in a tidy and an orderly manner. You may also consider the idea of floating shelves which will ensure that you efficiently use your space.

Increase the entry of natural light into your tiny house by using simple window dressing. For your windows go for curtains that can be swept from the window to allow in light or go for roller or Roman blinds. Also, consider using full-length curtains as they will help create an illusion of space by drawing eyes upwards. Also using stripe design for your curtains may help add to the appearance of space. Also, consider adding well laid out furniture and large wall mirrors to your decorative design to help add harmony to your tiny home.

Furniture

For your small home choosing the right furniture can be the difference between your houses feeling comfortable or cramped. Here are some great furniture that you should consider for your tiny home:

☐ Pedestal table

This is a simple round table with a small pedestal base that can easily fit into your small living area. Being a round table you will have no problem dealing with sharp corners. You also get the freedom to squeeze more people around the table.

☐ Stack of stools.

This is great furniture for when you have visitors around. A stack of stools does not occupy a lot of space and can easily be hidden in a corner until when you have visitors for you to unstick them for use.

☐ Small armchairs.

For your small Pedestal table consider having small armchairs that you can easily stack together when not in use. This will help you effectively use space in your house as you only unstuck the comfortable armchairs when you need to use them.

☐A small personal table

If you work from your tiny house then you will need a small personal table for you do your job effectively. If you work from a laptop and your office table needs are basic then you may be innovative with this and consider going for a folding desk that you set up when you want to work and then fold it and tuck it away when it is time to  do other things. This will help free up a lot of your floor space and make your house appear more organized.

☐A multi-purpose bed

Typically you only sleep for a small fraction of your day. You can make use of the space your bed occupies by having a multipurpose bed. For example, you could have a multipurpose bed that is both a bed and a sofa so that you can fold it and use it as a seat during the day especially when you have more visitors or when you have to sit in comfort and art night you use it as a bed.

## ☐Folding dining table

This is another great piece of furniture that will save you a lot of space. Given that you only eat three times a day, having a foldable dining table is a great idea for your tiny house. It takes less space is only used a few times a day and leaves your small house looking big throughout the day.

## Appliances

You've spent what feels like innumerable weeks laying the foundation of your tiny house, framing, roofing, sheathing, trimming and insulating your small house and you have at long last achieved goal of building your own tiny house and now you are on the final stage of furnishing your home. But, which small house apparatuses would it be advisable for you to pick? Which ones will serve the needs of your small house way of life the best?

Other than furniture you need a number of appliances to make your tiny house more comfortable. The following are important appliances you should consider when moving to your new tiny home:

☐Small Flat Screen TV

You need some form of entertainment in your new small house. A TV is popular in many homes and having it will help open the door of entertainment in your tiny home. Having a small flat screen TV will help you listen to music, watch movies and get informed of what is happening around you while still saving a lot of space. Having a TV does not mean that you will spend a lot of money on cable TV, you still find a lot of entertaining programs of public channels and this will help you save a lot of money. If Saving money is not your key priority then you may go for a laptop and then watch videos online and stream news and other TV programs over the internet.

## ☐Refrigerators

Choices for small house apparatuses, particularly fridges, are various and knowing which one to put your well-earned money into can be a challenge so how about we take a look at the different considerations to remember before settling on any particular choice. The principal thing to check is your electricity source and if your small house will be connected to a grid or will be powered by a solar system. In spite of what majority of the people think, fridges really represent a noteworthy burden to a solar system and use an average of almost

1kWh every day (350 kWh every year) for an 18 c.f. unit.

The next consideration relates to estimating the size of a fridge and knowing what number of cubic feet will meet your specific needs. The majority of us have been brought up to believe that a bigger unit is preferred yet all the more frequently; it winds up with spoiled foods because we store more than we need in it. Then again, a refrigerator that is too small can turn into a source of frustration especially when you can't store in it, sufficient foods for your needs.

Alternate consideration revolves around your budget, lifestyle and personal preferences. Luckily there are a lot of choices out there to serve your needs. so take your time study the market and find the most perfect refrigerator that will meet your needs while saving you space in your tiny house.

☐Ranges and Ovens

Different alternatives exist with regards to cooking surfaces and which one you pick depends on upon what your source of heat (electric or propane), the number of people you consistently cook for, and the amount of space you can save for a range or an oven.

When choosing which unit to buy, it's imperative for you to be honest and sensible about what your requirements really are. if you can, visit or lease a house on AirBnB or any other place that has a range the size that you are thinking about and check whether that unit addresses your specific needs. You might be shocked at how a small range can be efficient in preparing even a large feast

Some of the important consideration when choosing the kind of range or over to buy includes

☐ Source of heart (electricity or Propane)

Making these decision boils down the whether you are connected to a grid or you use solar panels. Ranges and ovens that use electricity represent a heavy burden to your power source and unless you are connected to a reliable grid I will recommend that you go for the propane appliances. What this means is that if you intend to move around with your tiny home more regularly then you should prioritize going for propane appliances.

☐The size of the range or the oven

The size of your cooking appliance is also an important fact in making your choice of which to acquire. The size also corresponds the overall floor size of your home. If you have a smaller home of below 400 square feet then you will want a much smaller range or oven than when your home if above 500 square feet. In addition, if you eat outside most of the times then a smaller cooking appliance is perfect for you as opposed when you mainly cook in your home.

☐**Dishwashers**

Many people who embrace tiny house living often choose to wash their dishes with hands in order to save space and money by not buying a dishwasher. But not everyone is a fan of washing dishes with hand. If you fall into this category then using a dishwasher is the perfect opportunity. There are a lot of small sizes to medium size dishwashers that can perfectly fit into your tiny house and leave a lot of space. For example, Drawer style dishwashers are low profile systems and offer a lot of help when it comes to washing small loads of glass where and dishes.

# Chapter 12: Building the right mentality for tiny house living

Living in a tiny house is not for everyone. But then the things you can learn from tiny house owners and the benefits you can derive from tips and tricks they've acquired throughout the years is priceless.

If there's anything that you immediately notice with tiny houses; it's the fact that these houses are so clean and uncluttered!

Now look at your current living space.

How much stuff do you have? Is there stuff in your house that you possess that you've already forgotten about? Do you really need two oversized couches?

What about the rooms, how many rooms in your house are seldom used?

We live in a world where capitalism has promoted the growth of consumerism resulting in a lot of excess which we unconsciously support. Advertising companies convince us that we need this thing and that thing even if we really don't. The next thing you know, you're in the mall picking up more stuff to clutter up your house!

And how do we deal with clutter?

We store it in our basements or attics and let it store dust over the years. If that's not enough, we go out and rent storage space and let it collect dust there!

That's a lot of wasted space and money.

Living in a tiny house forces you to rethink your buying decisions as well as how you store things. If you've ever been in a tiny house or talked to a tiny house owner you'll hear things like: "only the essential things go into my house" or "I practice a minimalistic lifestyle" or "one in and one out".

These are all statements that depict a minimalistic lifestyle which seem to go hand in hand with living in a tiny house. You can't afford to have any clutter in a space as tiny as that of a tiny house!

Now that doesn't mean you have to move out of your house now and take up residence in a tiny house because you've got all that clutter right now. You can actually take the time after you read this eBook to re-assess the things you own. Take a good hard look and be very honest with yourself if the things around you are the things you actually need.

So how can you get rid of all this clutter?

Well we've mentioned some tips in the previous chapter on how to de-clutter your home. You could hold a garage sale and make a mint off of the things you don't need any more or you could do something nice for the world and give away your stuff to charity.

You can also take on a paradigm shift and change your buying habits, adapt a somewhat minimalistic lifestyle and stop comparing yourself with the next door neighbors.

A further step into the tiny house mentality for normal homeowners would be to become more self-sufficient. You have a yard that goes along with that big house, right? Why don't you plant some vegetables in it? You'll be able to save up on your food expenses that way.

You can also install commercially available solar panels to start collecting energy from the sun and cut your energy bills down.

For more information as to how you can save up even if you don't move to a smaller house, try talking to people who are part of the tiny house movement. They have excellent tips and strategies which you can employ in your search for a better quality of life even if you live in a normal sized house!

It isn't just about the size of the house; it's about living big.

# Chapter 13: Design Ideas and Tips

Everyone thinks of designing their own house at one time or another, but they never get the chance. However, because of the uniqueness of tiny houses, it is possible to be as creative as you want to be. There are quite a few steps in designing a house from scratch, so it pays to study up on ways to get everything you want in your tiny house. Just like most great ideas, tiny houses start with a floor plan. You can simplify this if you purchase premade floor plans but if you have a little talent in this area, it is possible to draw one up for yourself. When it comes to choosing the right design for your new home, think about what will best suit the kind of lifestyle you want to lead. You can find plans that can meet every possible need you might have. Here are a few design ideas to get you started:

Design for Singles

The Diogone - an 8x10 house designed and named after the Greek philosopher Diogenes. Its minimalist style has everything that a single person could possibly want for comfort. The wooden saddle roofed house is completely self-sufficient with its own solar power and water collection system. That means if you park it in the right location you won't ever have to hook up to public utilities or pay a utility bill again. You can get one as small as 160 square feet up to 360 square feet.

Design for Couples

The Tarleton Tiny House made by Tumbleweed. The 120 square foot design comes fully equipped with everything a couple might need. The kitchen is actually a reasonable and functional size, a bathroom complete with shower, a sleeping loft, and a sitting room for entertaining visitors.

Design for Families

The most common argument usually launched against tiny houses is that they are not suitable for families. However, depending on the design, a small house could work very well for families. Driftwood Homes in South Carolina created the Indigo, a nice two-bedroom structure with an extra-large loft built on a 24-foot trailer. The entire 280 square feet tiny house even showcases a sitting area for entertaining. The design has a really open feeling, making it look much larger than it really is.

Design Idea for Seniors

To take advantage of the space, many tiny homes build upward to make room for extra bedrooms. However, tiny house designs for seniors tend to be single level to avoid the need for climbing. These designs usually have the entryway along the side of the house and a full-size bed or pull out sofa for sleeping. They can even be designed with extra wide entryways for those who may need to maneuver with mobility devices.

## Customized Design Ideas

One way you can be absolutely sure that your tiny house will meet all of your needs and expectations is to have a customized design. You'll work directly with a consultant who not only understands all the legal aspects of building a tiny house, but also all of the construction options available. You can even choose between a full or partial build to get exactly what you desire.

## Interior Design Tips

Unlike a traditional house where you may have more than enough space to move around and store things, the space in a tiny house will at a premium. Things you might take for granted in a regular house must be carefully accounted for in a tiny house.

Choose lighter colors to give you a feeling of more space. Darker colors make your small house feel closed in, but lighter colors will brighten the place up and give it an open feeling, especially if you have a lot of windows.

When choosing furniture, think multipurpose. Every item you use should be able to service your needs differently. For example, a Murphy bed will make sure you have a comfortable place to sleep at night but if there is a desk attached to the other side, you have the incentive to get up and make your bed up in the morning and a place to work during the day.

Use smaller tables. It will give you more freedom of movement so you won't feel confined.

Glass walls that allow you to extend your space outside perhaps onto a deck or a patio will open up your space in a big way. Because the line of sight goes through the windows to the outdoors, the house will seem much larger than it really is. Use creative storage solutions; tables that have storage spaces underneath, baskets that can be hidden away, and stairs that hide cubbies can allow you to store away lots of things when not in use. Use fold down furniture. Desks and tables can easily be converted to other types of furniture when needed and put away when not in use.

Make good use of wall space. By hanging items on the walls, you'll eliminate a lot of the clutter that can quickly accumulate in your home.

## Chapter 14: Utilities and appliances

Install the rough pumbing first to prevent effects on the electrical wires in case of accidents. This also involves making the decision to install the showers, tubs, toilets and sinks based on the design of the house. This also includes such electrical appliances as refrigerators, dishwashers, laundy machines among others.

Depending on the amount of water that is required in the house for use, ensure that you select the appropriate size of water heaters. Make sure that you set standards for the house purpose based on the budget that you have.

 The next factor is gas and electricity. This involves making the appropriate choice of the lighting that we intend to use in the house to ensure simplicity and efficiency.

Consider cheaper alternatives when it comes to the utilities and appliances that you install in your tiny house. This includes the use of solar panels which is great and costs effective alternative to electricity.

Wall and flooring

Once the tiny house skeleton is done, and the utilities and appliances have been installed, the next thing is to install floors and walls. The choice of time of installation is often dependent on the terrain and climatic condition of the location you chose to construct your tiny house. Usually, the floors come first to make it easy for movements within the house.

Also, this involves making the decision on what woods to use for the floor among othr materials such as tiles, stone, and vinyl. However, if your desired floors are carpeting, then this is done at the end to avoid messing it up.

For the walls, it is important the similar concept is applied. Remember that appliances will be installed in the house and so it is important that you leave spaces around the designated ares ideal for the installation.

Décor

This is the point where you are ready to install various appliances and décor materials in the house. This is where we often have to insert our creativity skills to work for us. It is important that you ensure that the windows and the doors are large enough to allow for entry of appliances.

When you are working on the counters and the sinks around your tiny house, pay attention to the rough plumbing so that there are proper dimensions of the lines.

It is also at this point that we decide where the extra storages and utility spaces go. Ensure that the appliances coincide well with the rough plumbing and electric wiring. Choose the appropriate kind of cabinetry that will work well with your needs. Ensure that all your décor ca match up with future décor while staying within the range of the budget.

Ensure that you have the better understanding of the appliance regulations that your country might have about stoves and their safety use. This is based on the fact that certain locations require specialized materials installed to surround the stove and reduce the risk of fires.

For the extra rooms that you have designed in your tiny house, add a specialized detail to the room to enhance the décor and the design of the final product. Ensure that such details as lighting in the closets is addressed adequately. The windows should also complement the prevailing climatic conditions in the place the tiny house has been built.

Finishing touch

Based on the fact that the design of your tiny huse was fun, this is the most fun part of it all. After ensuring that the plumbing, electricity and other utilities in the tiny house are working efficiently, it is time to paint the walls, add in furniture, and decorate the tiny house with a sense of our personalities.

This includes such things as the addition of tiles around the kitchen cooking appliances or mosaic designs in the bathroom. The carpeting for those that desire it can be completed at this point in construction. This is the point when you can give your tiny house a wipe-down.

This is through installation of décor lightings such as chandeliers as well as adding a little sense of décor detail to the exterior of the house such as flower beds and potted plants.

# Chapter 15: Principles and Steps behind a Successful Minimalist Life

Before we look into the different steps that are involved in decluttering your home, let us take a look at the different principles based upon which the foundation of minimalism is formulated. There are four key principles when it comes to achieving a successful and decluttered lifestyle.

**Principles**

Collecting the Necessary Data

The best way of collecting data is by making a list of all the items that you use or need in your life. For instance, if you want to declutter your closet or wardrobe in your bedroom, then take everything out of the cupboard and make a list of everything that you come across in that cupboard or closet.

Choosing the Items

Now that you have finished making a list of the items, you can separate them into different categories on paper, or you can even do it physically to save time. Choose the things that you need and segregate the things that you don't need or use anymore. If you are not sure about any particular item in the list, put it in a "pending" or "unsure" pile.

Eliminating the Rest

Throw away everything that is in your "unnecessary" pile. These are the things that you do not use or need anymore. You may find it very hard doing this initially, but you need to persevere through it and grit your teeth through the initial stages. If you choose to hold on to these things, you will never be able to declutter your house successfully.

Reorganizing the Remaining Items

Now that you have segregated and got rid of the things that you don't need, it is now time to reorganize everything that is left. The organization is the most important thing when it comes to minimizing your life, and consequently, your home, from going back to being cluttered again. If everything you use is arranged neatly in the appropriate storage spaces, everything looks neater and more appealing to you. Therefore, if you do finish removing clutter, you do not want to spoil it by cluttering it up again. If you keep cramming things into a small space, you will never stop adding things because, in the back of your mind, you feel that things are already messy anyway and that adding one or two more things will never make a difference in your eyes.

**Steps**

Now that we have been introduced to the different principles behind minimalism, it is time to learn about the different steps that are involved in implementing these basic principles into your life.

Step 1: Believe That it is Possible

If you do not believe that you can lead a minimalist lifestyle, you will never be able to implement the principles that are involved in leading a minimalist lifestyle, and you will have a tough time working through the entire process. Since you are already here reading this book, I think it is safe to assume that you believe in the minimalist lifestyle.

You will need some help to get started initially, so consider enlisting the help of a friend or family member. However, there might be a few of you who may be coming across the principles of minimalist living for the first time, and this might be intriguing for them, especially when it comes to the implementation of these principles. Coincidentally these people might also be the ones who are sick of leading a cluttered lifestyle but do not know how to go about decluttering their homes.

Many people who meet these criteria might have completely given up hope of ever clearing out the clutter from their houses. For these people, the very first step of the process is to believe in yourself and have the confidence that you can do it. You will never be able to declutter your home if you do not believe that you can get it done. You need to have the mental resolve and put it in your mind that minimalism is possible, and that you can do it. Every great journey begins with a single step, and this is that single step that begins your journey into the world of minimalist living. Once you have made the initiative to take the first step, taking the second step becomes a much easier thing to do.

## Step 2: Getting Rid of the Excess

Clutter becomes more and more prominent in your house if you have the habit of collecting and holding onto things. When you focus your energy and give more importance to a smaller number of things in your life, then it becomes much easier to curb the amount of clutter that is in your home. Once you start believing in the different principles of minimalism, the next step of the process is getting rid of all the excess things that you own or deem unimportant.

These excess things (including people, situations, and sentiments) take up precious time, energy, and effort from your life. In order to get rid of all these extra things from your life, it will be very useful and effective if you develop boundaries and a definition of importance, which should allow you to separate clutter from the things that are important.

Having excess could mean having too many things that look similar to each other, or are similar in function or the things that have no function in your life. It could also be the things that don't appeal to you or that you don't love using anymore. We all have passing tendencies and fads that we follow momentarily, and during this, we end up accumulating a lot of things that we might never use after a certain point in our life. This could be because of any number of reasons but may have just begun to irritate you.

If you have developed a clear definition of what is important and what is not, you can start removing the things that fall into the latter category. In some cases, it may be very easy to define what is important and what is not, and getting rid of the excess things becomes an easy thing to do. For instance, if you have dressers or drawers that are full of clutter such as used batteries, rubber bands, defunct earphones, and other knick-knacks like that, a quick sort through will highlight exactly what to get rid of.

If your cupboards are jam-packed with both old clothes and new, it is time to segregate the things that you don't use and throw them out. However, there will also be some instances when decluttering can become a hassle. For example, if you want to declutter a larger space such as the attic, the garage, or the basement, it may take you a lot of time to pile everything up and sort it out.

The most difficult items to get rid of are the ones with sentimental value attached to them. The old family heirlooms or keepsakes that were handed down to you by your grandmother, which are broken and not usable anymore, will always stay put in your life because you cannot muster up the resolve that is necessary to throw them away. However, you will have to make that decision at one point in time or another because you will eventually run out of storage space after a certain point in time. It is easier to make a tough decision right away instead of letting things fester and reach the saturation point before you make your decision.

Lots of people also have a very hard time getting rid of things like old books, and if you are adamant when it comes to holding on to your book collection, you should consider finding a permanent storage space for them so that they don't clutter up your house. It is important to keep in mind that while you are decluttering your home, stay away from things that belong to other people who might be living with you (a roommate or a family member). You might feel the temptation to chuck something out, but you cannot do that, simply because it does not belong to you.

Getting rid of the excess in your house is easier if you do it a bit at a time. Don't try tackling it all at once. Always start small, and once you familiarize yourself gradually and feel the smaller victories, you will develop the confidence to take on bigger and more complicated projects. If you find it very difficult to throw away things or get rid of them, try finding an intermediate point or a middle ground. You could begin by packing away all your extras into a box and using a storage unit to keep the things that you don't need until you bring yourself to the point of making a decision and getting rid of them.

Step 3: Develop the Habit of Decluttering Regularly

The secret behind sustaining a minimalist lifestyle is to implement small changes and practices that allow you to keep clutter under control. If you make a conscious and active effort towards removing clutter regularly, leading a minimalist life becomes easier than leading a normal life. If you are not removing clutter and simply moving it around from one corner of the house to another, your habits will have no effect when it comes to alleviating the clutter in your life.

Once you develop the habit of regularly clearing away the excess that builds up in your home, you will be able to effectively hone your decluttering practices and develop your own process that works most efficiently for you. Once you get a taste of the freedom that comes with living a minimalist lifestyle, going back to living life the way you used to will seem like a bleak and unappealing prospect.

Step 4: Regulate the Hoarding of Items

In today's world, you cannot live without consuming items. Consumption is something that cannot be avoided. However, we can try to control the amount we consume. If you manage to regulate the number and ways items enter your possession, then you can easily manage your clutter.

To decrease the entry of clutter into your house and life, you need to change your mindset. You need to start evaluating the items you purchase in a different way. You firstly need to accept that each item you purchase is actually more expensive than its cost price. It has the added price of occupying precious space, time, and energy in your life. Therefore, you need to ask yourself a number of questions before buying an item. You need to be a hundred percent sure that you need this item.

You also need to make sure that your home has a place for this item. If not, you should plan to throw something out to make space for this one. If you just keep buying items without throwing other ones out, you will keep accumulating things. This method of questioning your purchases isn't meant to stop you from buying things ever. That is not possible. We live in a consumer world. It is extremely difficult to live without buying anything. These questions exist to make you question the necessity of the items you are buying.

Creative Ways to Declutter

• There are many ways of working through the things in your home and making everything more organized. There are numerous sites and blogs that can be found on the Internet which give different tips and tricks when it comes to decluttering, the most popular one being

Zen Habits by Leo Babua. Pick something that you think should work for you well, and begin your journey into the minimalist lifestyle.

• Take a moment each day or each week where you take a large bin bag and fill it with things that you don't need. Just look around your space and see the various things that you use, the things that you don't require, and get rid of all the things that do not affect your life anymore.

# Chapter 16: How to Begin Living in a Tiny House?

It might not be everyone's preference to live in a house whose size is smaller than a walk-in closet, but those who choose these small houses reap many benefits not only to themselves but also, for their environment. However, in order to live effectively and comfortably in a tiny home, you need to plan adequately and prepare yourself for every odd, which may come your way. It may not be easy, especially if you're used to living in 'mansions', but it's not very hard. Make your living enjoyable, as opposed to a confining one using these tips:

Do your research

Tiny homes are available in many types and can range from 9 sq ft. up to 837 sq ft. Moreover, different houses have different designs such as the traditionally built tiny houses to the ultra-modern designs. Other houses even incorporate off-the-grid designs such as composting toilets, rainwater collection and solar/wind power. Do your homework and come up with the design that best suits your needs.

Determine the paraphernalia you need

Most people prefer a quite, dry, comfortable place to sleep, lie or sit down. Others want a place to prepare, eat and store food for future consumption. But for this purposes to be fulfilled you need to have the necessary tools and equipment such as clothes, dryer, washer, a refrigerator etc. Therefore, your dwelling's floor space should allow the combing of all these appliances to avoid congestion.

Consider the benefits of a tiny house

As we mentioned earlier, "living small" has many benefits; greener environment footprint, lower energy bills, less unneeded appliances and clothes pack-rating and less space for you to clean. Other tiny houses are mobile; therefore, you need not sell your home at the time of relocating. If the several benefits which can be attained by living in tiny houses don't impress you, then tiny houses are not your type.

Realize that the cost per square feet of small houses is higher

The cost is higher when compared to larger houses. This is because small area designs are more complex since items should be custom made in order to utilize all the space accordingly. Also, full sized appliances, in most cases, are cheaper than compact appliances. If you're building or designing your house on trailer beds, then you should keep plumbing (black water and grey water disposal and storage) into account.

Decide whether you want a ready built house, or you want to build one from your plan

The decision also includes whether you want a used house or a new one. But the cheapest solution is to go for a well-maintained travel trailer or used RV. The advantage of buying a house is that it has already been designed and constructed. However, the disadvantage is that you can't fully customize the house to your wants and needs.

Pare down belongings

We spend a large percentage of our time wearing very few clothes, as opposed to the number of clothes in our wardrobe. Therefore, we can make our life simpler by disposing off or getting rid of the wasted percentage; less indecision about dressing and less laundry. Instead of having 3 game stations, a VCR, 3 TVs, DVD, 2 computers, and Blue-Ray, you can buy a computer; use the flat screen monitor to substitute the TVs and transfer movies to your hard drive.

Be creative about multi-function furniture and storage

You could design a bed whih has storage drawers underneath such as clothes storage drawers. Even a built-in sofa can be used to store many things in the space underneath. You can make a table with shelves underneath the table surface for storage purposes. Use deep and broad drawers and shelves and ceiling and wall mounted items, the wasted space portion around, below, and above the items edges (due to falling-off-the-edge risk or packing geometry). Consider metal furniture so as

to minimize the space occupied by the
furniture.

# Chapter 17: Decluttering and Guilt

Part of successful tiny house living is based on the functionality of your home. So far the discussion has been in how to reduce the need for a mortgage or how to live without spending a great deal on your tiny house life. Now, you will want to focus on the comfort of your home. The items you are able to bring into your tiny home are based on space, weight, and functionality.

A person with a stationary tiny home does not have to worry about weight, but you will need to be concerned with space and functionality. There are innovative organization methods, but "know yourself." Are you the type of person who will put away things after you have used them or do you let things pile up? Are you truly a person who can make your bed every day, when the necessity is there or will you avoid such a chore?

Living in a tiny house requires a hyper-organized and a proactive nature. If you cannot keep your space clean now, how likely will you be able to do so if you bring in a lot of things?

There are definitely rules you must follow to declutter your life for going tiny, as well as to ensure you do not feel guilty when you get rid of something.

Decluttering Rules

If you have not used the item within the last six months, it goes.

Any duplicates of books, photos, or other items, you keep one.

Take photos of nostalgic keepsakes, then donate or sell them.

If you don't like it, and it was a present, it goes.

Find a home for all items or design your house to have a place for all items.

Start putting things away now, before your tiny house is built. Practice keeps you in an appropriate routine.

Think "someone else needs this more than I do." It helps you eliminate things you no longer use, and cannot take with you into your tiny home.

If you wouldn't buy the item today, it goes. If an item no longer fits into your décor, home size, or preferences, do not keep it.

Examine your spending habits. Do you truly need something that will add to your tiny house clutter?

Follow the rules and keep repeating them until you can eliminate all but the essential items.

Getting Rid of the Guilt Rules

Do you truly like an item you own that someone gave you?

Is the heirloom something you treasure because you find it attractive?

Have you ever given a gift that wasn't right, and wished the person would donate it or return it to the store?

If you have an item that someone gave you and you like it, keep it, if it is something you can fit into your tiny house. If the gift is unlikable because it is not your style or you find it ugly, remember, "It is your life!" Sometimes gift giving goes wrong. You cannot let the guilt weigh you down.

A coworker brought back soap from their month long trip. The person who received the gift is allergic to perfume. Should that person suffer the allergic reaction, and keep the soap? No. Should they feel guilty about giving it to someone else or getting rid of it? Of course, not. They also shouldn't make the gift giver feel guilty by not accepting the gift and giving a solid reason as to why.

You have honest justifications for getting rid of gifts others have given you, for taking pictures of heirlooms or passing them on to other family, as well as understanding that you too have given wrong gifts.

As long as you can accept the truth that not all things can be liked or enjoyed, you can donate, sell or trash items you do not need, want, or cannot fit into your tiny home lifestyle.

# Chapter 18: BUILDING A FOUNDATION

Before we look at the unique designs that a tiny house can have, we have to learn how to build a foundation. After all, our foundation is what our design will be based off of.

Choosing a window:

There is no simple way to go about selecting a window for your tiny house. With so many available on the market, some people have trouble finding one that would suit their style. However, it definitely helps to become more familiar with the popular styles of windows that are available today.

**Sliding Window** – Sliding windows open by using two sashes that slide right past one another. These are nice windows if you want to be able to quickly open up for a quick breeze. The only drawback to sliding windows are that they can easily be tampered with. They can often be opened from the outside, which can cause a bit of concern for some people.

**Bay Window** – Bay windows are a window space that projects outward from the main walls of a building. It essentially forms a bay where the window resides. Personally,

I don't recommend installing a bay window. I'm not sure as to how a large bay window could find a place inside a tiny house. Keep note that if you decide to install a bay window, you will be changing the shape of your house. You may need to redesign the floor, walls, and roof of the house to compensate for that.

**Awning Window –** An awning window is a casement window that is hung horizontally and hinged on the top so that it can swing back and forth like an awning. A lot of us are familiar with this design because awning windows were the window of choice for most commercial structure post World War II. Awning windows aren't as common in today's building structure, but they can still be found in basement settings. In a tiny house, they may just be what you need in a sleeping loft to assure that the proper amount of breeze passes through.

**Storm Windows** – Storm windows are windows that are mounted outside or inside of the main glass windows of a house. They are basically a second pane of glass used to insulate your house during its colder months. My advice is to avoid using storm windows since they are not a strong suit for tiny house living.

**Skylights** – Skylights are light transmitting windows on the top of the ceiling. They let light pass through the roof for day lighting purposes. In my opinion, skylights are great for tiny house living. They let natural light pass through without sacrificing any privacy. This can make your tiny house have a more "surreal" feeling.

Heating your house:

As with the case of the construction of a tiny house, trying to find how to heat it can be difficult due to the lack of available space. Finding a heating unit that would actually work in a tiny house ended taken many hours of research, visiting showrooms, and networking with other tiny house owners that had to face the same problem. The challenge that I personally faced was finding a propane heater than didn't require electricity usage, that needed minimal space so that I could place it in the corner of a small area, and that would output the right amount of heat without cooking us alive. The other difficulty was also finding one that was reasonably priced and could manually let you set the temperature. I ended up using the Hampton H27 as my heater, but it will differ from person to person depending on what you want.

The first thing you should consider is how powerful you want your heater to be. You can use free online BTU calculators to do so. BTU is a unit of heat that's commonly used in the heating and cooling industry. The acronym stands for British thermal unit and most heaters are rated in BTUs. Finding the right heater for your tiny house is all about discovering a heater that will provide you with just the right amount of BTUs.

The next step is to choose which type of heater you want for your tiny house. Normal central heat or large wood stoves produce way too much heat for the small space. But don't worry. I will show you a few options that you can use.

**Electric** – If you have a constant electricity supply, this type of heater will be idealistic. There are many small electric heaters that work quite well in small spaces. For example, you can even find some at your local supermarkets like WalMart. Electric heaters also cost much less than your typical wood, gas, or propane ones (a typical one costs approximately $100). I definitely recommend getting an electric heater if you have a constant supply of electricity.

Propane — This is probably the second most popular type of heater for tiny houses. Propane heaters can be thought up as a small fireplace. The combustion process is isolated from the insides of the structure by the vent design. Also, the built in blower provides a good amount of circulation. The heater is often sold with accessories that include a stainless steel chimney and a stainless steel backing plate. Propane heaters are often more expensive. For instance, the Newport

Propane Fireplace costs around $1040 give or take.

Gas – Gas stoves are also a popular alternative for heating a tiny house. This is what I used for my tiny house. Several people have told me the same as well. Kerosene burns really hot and is approximately 90% efficient, according to a local gas supplier that I talked to. In terms of BTU output, kerosene produces more than propane, but it's not as environmental friendly (they do make filters to reduce emissions though). Kerosene is the cheaper option compared to propane, but it isn't as easy to find. Cost range can be quite drastic ($100 - $700, depending on which one you get).

Wood – Unlike the other alternative heating sources, there is a "home" feeling to a wood stove that just isn't there with the other ones. A wood stove can work just as well as the propane or gas, but it's often a lot messier, with ash falling through the stove pen, and wood chips/barks trailing in the wood. Wood stoves can also be quite expensive as well ($600 - $1000, depending on model and make).

Finding and using materials to build house:

I often took pride in recycling, reclaiming, and reusing many of the materials that I bought for the construction of my tiny house. But where did I get the materials for this project?

Well, after scourging the shelves of home depot, Craigslist, and many other sources, I found that the best way to get materials was to collect supplies from existing construction projects, soon to be demolished houses, and people's junk piles that they would happily get rid of. Because of this, I was able to create a manageable budget since buying everything directly from an official supplier would likely have cost me twice as much, or even more. And in my opinion, it's without a doubt more interesting to scavenge existing infrastructure for parts that aren't needed anymore.

If you are like me, perhaps you don't know where to look for these reusable/recycled materials. Here are a few tips that you can use for finding materials to use for building your tiny house.

Urban decay areas – If you live in or live nearby a city and have access to a salvage yard, then you won't have too much difficulty finding scrap pieces of materials to build your house off of. They get loads of construction "waste," which really aren't wastes since they can be reused. Existing projects that have extra material or have materials that they don't need will often ship it to these salvage yards.

Frequently visit shops – There is no substitute for regularly showing up at stores and looking at their inventories. Store owners/managers will often give you "top priority treatment" since they see you coming often. That will definitely help you on your mission to gather materials.

Switching up suppliers — Look at other external sources. Perhaps you frequently visit Home Depot. Look on Craigslist. Perhaps you've looked on Craigslist and still couldn't find what you needed. Then post an ad in the newspaper classified stating exactly what you're looking for. The key here is to switch around and use many different sources. That way, you've covered everyone you can talk to.

Learn to say "No" - This may be one of the toughest things that you will have to face — learning to say no in the face of free materials. When you're building a house, you want quality materials. You don't want scrap pieces of wood found lieing around in the middle of a junkyard. Don't take material, or even buy material if you aren't certain that you will need it for your project. Remember that you're going to be living in that house.

Anchoring down house:

It's important to be able to anchor your house down into the ground. Perhaps you live in a region where there are constant hurricanes, or maybe tornadoes. Even though there is still a risk factor of being blown away, you want to minimize the risk on yourself. Always keep in mind that safety is your priority. There's no point in living in a tiny house if it isn't going to shelter you from storms.

If you're planning on living in a mobile tiny house, then check the tie-downs, which are the system of steel straps and anchors that is designed to keep your house in one place. Check it at least once per year to make sure that it doesn't wear off. If you live in an area with frequent hurricanes, check the tie-downs once before the hurricane season and once after. If repairs are required, then make them despite the expense. Your safety should be your priority.

But let's talk about how the anchoring system works. There are three primary parts to an anchoring system:

Anchors – These are steel rods that are several feet long. You can screw them into the ground. Only a few inches of the steel rods should be above the surface of the ground. We want to ensure that it maximizes its holding power just the way it's designed.

Steel straps – Steel straps allow you to fasten around the frame of a mobile house. These are attached to the anchors with adjustable bolts. Also, please note that it's difficult to guess how many straps there should be for your tiny house. The state standards and the numbers set by engineers have been constantly changing throughout the past couple decades.

Piers – Piers are what your tiny house will sit on. They're often made of concrete blocks stacked on top of a concrete pad.

To reiterate, please note that the purpose of anchoring down the house isn't for added stability, but to prevent heavy winds from making the structure unsafe. To avoid this, you will need to anchor your home down, especially if you live in areas with high amounts of hurricanes or tornadoes. According to mobile home manufacturers, a mobile house up to 40ft long should have two diagonal ties per side and three vertical ties per side.

**Installing the anchor** – To install anchors, there are several things you should do:

Level your tiny house – Make sure that the ground surface is leveled before you anchor your tiny house to the ground.

Determine type of soil – Depending on the foundation of the soil underneath you, some anchors will need to be deeper than others. For instance, some types of anchors will need to be installed five feet deep due to the weak foundation of the soil. For concrete, make sure that it's at minimum 4 inches deep.

Select anchor type – It's best to ask your supplier which anchor type will suit your tiny house the best. In most cases, your soil type will determine what type of anchor you need

Install your anchor – Again you should ask your supplier for advice on how to do this. Different anchors have different installation instructions. If you have a vertical tie-down, the anchor should be installed vertically. For diagonal tie downs, the anchor should be installed diagonally at the same angle that your tie-down is (so in most cases around 40-50 degrees). You can also pour concrete around the top of the anchor to ensure that the anchor hardens.

Adjust tensions — Adjust the tensions of the tie-down to make sure that your house has a good solid foundation. Make sure that it wouldn't have any chance of rocking back and forth, even during windy days. Don't fully adjust one side of your house, and then do the other. Do both sides at the same time.

# Conclusion

Moving to a tiny house is a great idea, but not something that works for just anybody. The secret to making a successful transition is to ensure that you are prepared for the huge change. It is not just about living in a smaller house. It is an entirely new lifestyle.

Your preparation includes doing research and being involved in the build. This does not mean literally hammering in a nail or screwing in a bolt, but rather being vocal about what you need and how you want to design the place. This will ensure that once you move in, everything will be as you wanted it to be.

Research will help you identify your purpose for going tiny. If it had been another family member's idea, then finding out more about tiny living will help you understand how it can work for you.

It is also a great idea to transition slowly. While waiting to move into your new home, you can start getting used to a simpler life by gradually adjusting your lifestyle. One simple example is to stop watching TV in your bedroom and use the one in the family room instead. You can also reduce your wardrobe slowly so you do not get shocked by the change.

Hopefully, this book has provided you with all the information you need to know about making the decision to go tiny and how to adjust to the change.